CROSBY, STILLS & NASH
FOR UKULELE

Cover photo © Getty Images / Henry Diltz / Contributor

ISBN 978-1-5400-2593-7

HAL•LEONARD®

Visit Hal Leonard Online at
www.halleonard.com

Contact us:
Hal Leonard
7777 West Bluemound Road
Milwaukee, WI 53213
Email: info@halleonard.com

In Europe, contact:
Hal Leonard Europe Limited
42 Wigmore Street
Marylebone, London, W1U 2RN
Email: info@halleonardeurope.com

In Australia, contact:
Hal Leonard Australia Pty. Ltd.
4 Lentara Court
Cheltenham, Victoria, 3192 Australia
Email: info@halleonard.com.au

Carry On

Words and Music by Stephen Stills

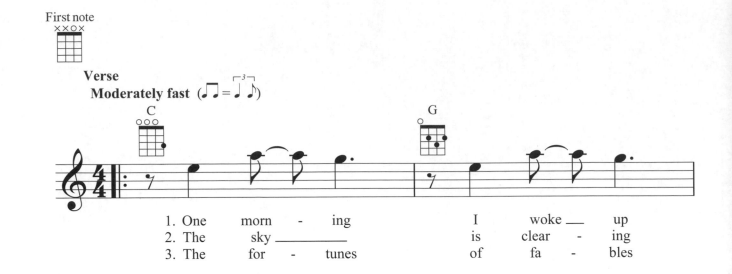

1. One morn - ing   I   woke ___ up
2. The sky ___   is   clear - ing
3. The for - tunes   of   fa - bles

and   I   knew ___   you   were   real - ly   gone. ___
and   the   night ___   has   cried ___   e - nough. ___
are ___   a - ble   to   see   the   stars. ___

A   new ___ day,   a   new ___ way
The   sun ___   he   comes, ___
Now   wit - ness   the   quick - ness

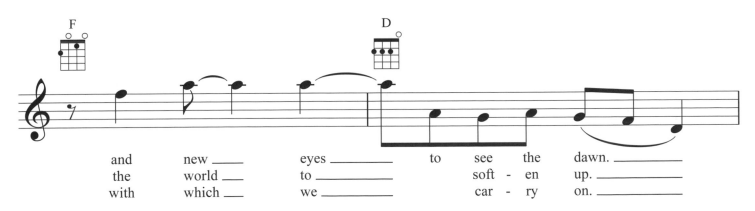

and   new ___   eyes ___   to   see   the   dawn. ___
the   world ___   to ___   soft - en   up. ___
with   which ___   we ___   car - ry   on. ___

Go your way _____ I'll go ___
Re - joice, ___ re - joice, ___ we have no ___
To sing ___ the blues, ___ you've got ___

___ mine, _____ and car - ry on. _____
___ choice _____ but to car - ry on. _____
___ to live the dues and car - ry on. _____

Play 3 times

Outro

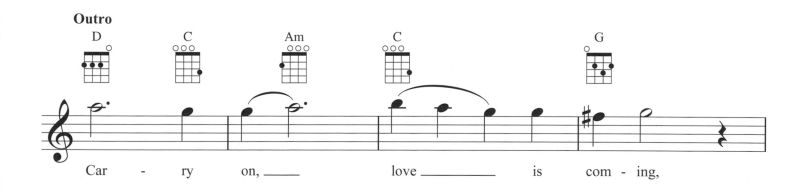

Car - ry on, ___ love _____ is com - ing,

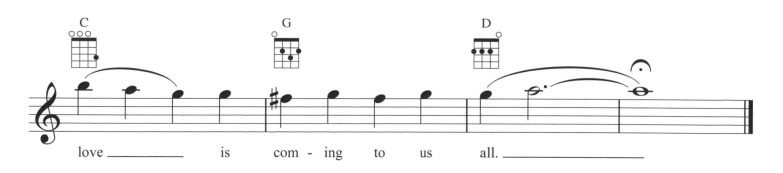

love _____ is com - ing to us all. _____

3

Daylight Again

Words and Music by Stephen Stills

Just a Song Before I Go

Words and Music by Graham Nash

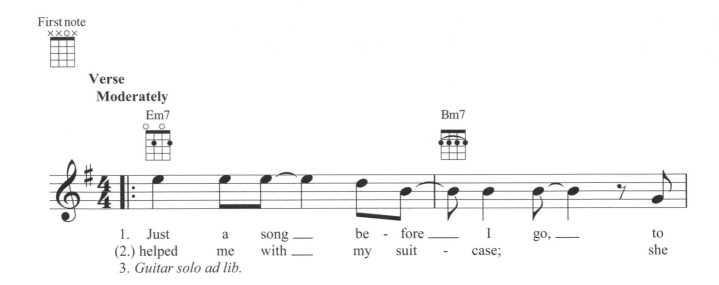

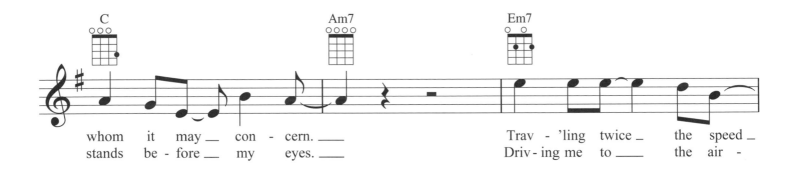

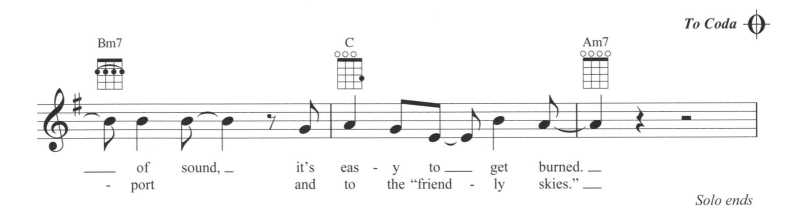

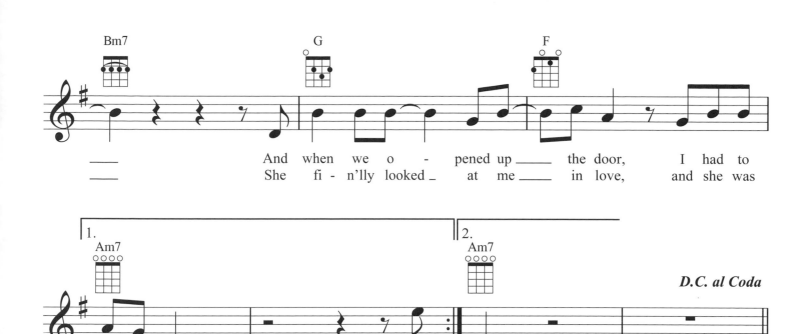

And when we o - pened up ____ the door, I had to
She fi - n'lly looked _ at me ____ in love, and she was

1.
Am7

be a - lone.

2.
Am7

D.C. al Coda

2. She gone.

Outro-Verse
Coda
Em7   Bm7

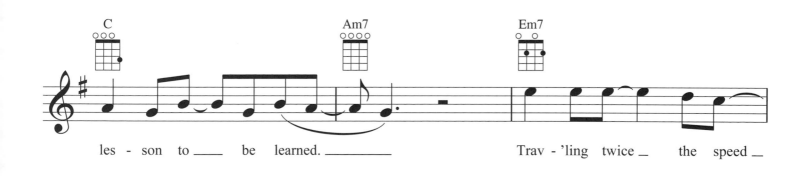

Just a song ____ be - fore ____ I go, ____ a

C   Am7   Em7

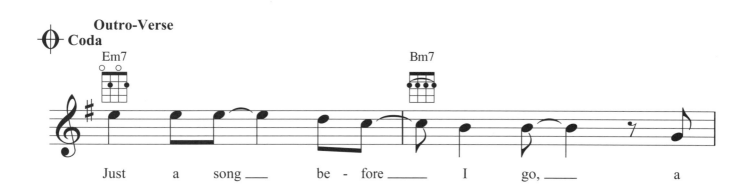

les - son to ____ be learned. _____ Trav - 'ling twice _ the speed _

Bm7   C   Em9
                                         5fr

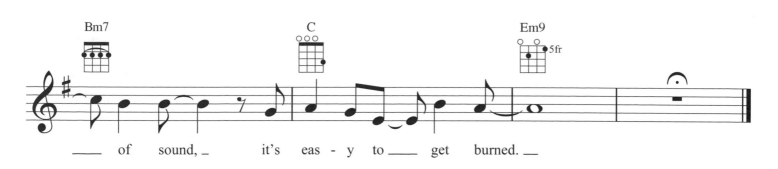

____ of sound, _ it's eas - y to ____ get burned. _

7

Long Time Gone

Words and Music by David Crosby

sure - ly won't ___ stand ___ the light of day. _____

And it ap - pears ___

And it ap - pears ___

D.S. al Coda

Coda

Bridge

Lead vocal ad lib. (Long _____ time _____ com -

- in'. ___ Long _____ time ___

_____ gone.) ___ But you know ___

the dark - est ho - ur _____ is

al - ways, _____ al - ways just be - fore __ the dawn. _____

Outro-Chorus

_____ And it ap - pears ____ to be ___ a long, _____ ap -

pears to be ___ a long, _____ ap - pears to be ___ a _____

long __ time, _____ such a long, ___ long, long, __ long

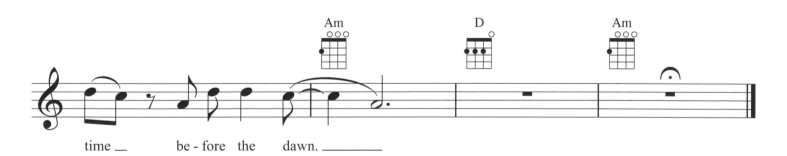

time __ be - fore the dawn. _____

Additional Lyrics

2. Speak out, you got to speak out against the madness.
You got to speak your mind, if you dare.
But don't, no don't, no, try to get yourself elected.
If you do, you had better cut your hair, mmm.

Love the One You're With

Words and Music by Stephen Stills

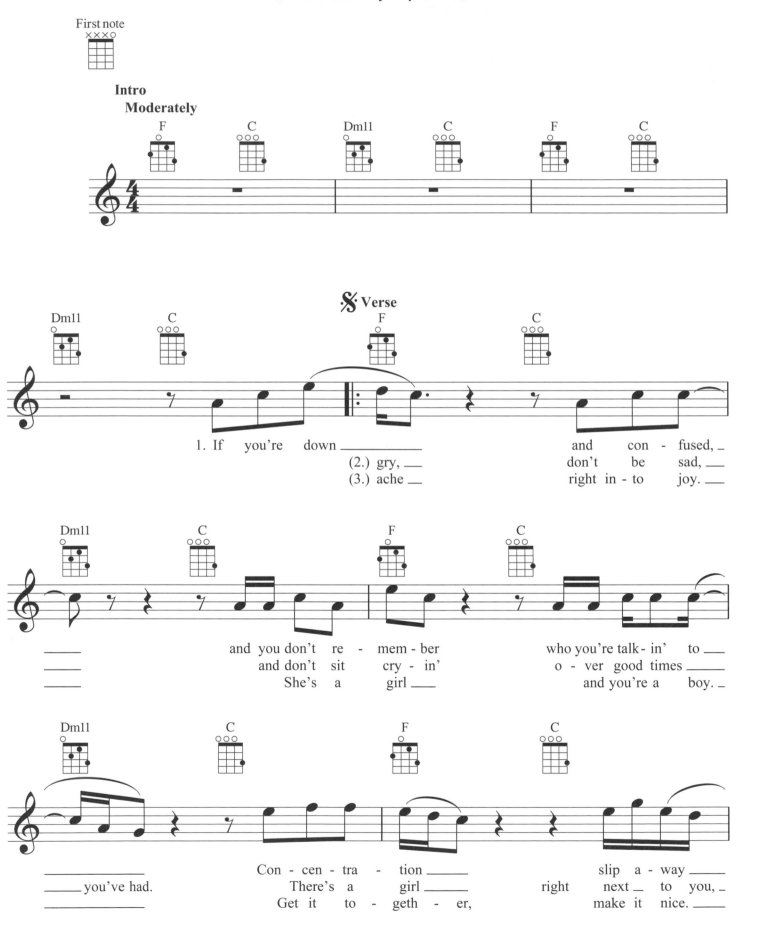

1. If you're down ___ and con- fused, ___ and you don't re- mem- ber who you're talk- in' to ___ ___ you've had. Con- cen- tra- tion ___ slip a- way ___

(2.) gry, ___ don't be sad, ___ and don't sit cry- in' o- ver good times ___ ___ There's a girl ___ right next ___ to you, ___

(3.) ache ___ right in- to joy. ___ She's a girl ___ and you're a boy. ___ Get it to- geth- er, make it nice. ___

Dm11   C   F   C

— 'cause your ba - by   is so far a - way —
— and she's just wait - in'   for some - thing to
— You ain't gon - na need   an - y more ad -

Dm11   C   **Chorus**   Am   G

——— do. ___ Well, there's a rose _____
vice. _ And there's a rose _____ } in the fist - ed
And there's a rose _____

F   Am   G

glove,   and the ea - gle flies   with the dove. _

F   Am   G

_____ And if __ you can't __ be   with the one __ you

F   F   C

love, _ hon - ey, love the one __ you're with.   Love the one __ you're with.

Love the one ___ you're with.   Love the one ___ you're with.

Bridge

2. Don't be an -   Do do   do ___   do   do ___   do   do   do.

Do do   do ___   do   do ___   do   do   do.   Do do   do ___   do   do ___   do   do   do.

Instrumental-Chorus

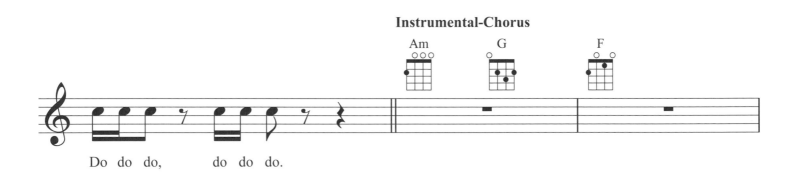

Do   do   do,   do   do   do.

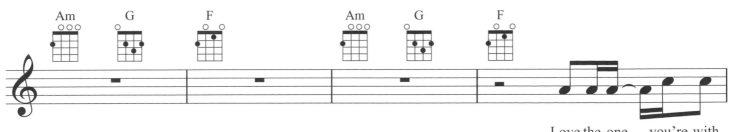

Love the one ___ you're with.

Love the one ___ you're with.   Love the one ___ you're with.

D.S. al Coda

Love the one ___ you're with.   3. Turn your heart -

⊕ **Coda**

Love the one ___ you're with.

Outro

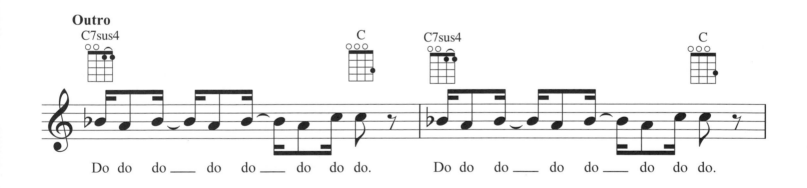

Do do do ___ do do ___ do do do.   Do do do ___ do do ___ do do do.

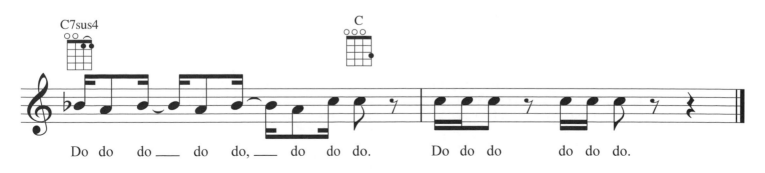

Do do do ___ do do, ___ do do do.   Do do do ___ do do do.

15

Marrakesh Express

Words and Music by Graham Nash

Verse
Light and rhythmic

1. Look - ing at _____ the world _ through the sun - set in _____ your eyes, _
2. Sweep - ing cob - webs from _ the edg - es of _____ my mind, _
3. Take the train _ to Cas - a - blan - ca go - ing south, _

trav - el - ing _____ the train _ through clear Mo - roc - can skies. _
had to get _____ a - way _ to see what we could find. _
blow - ing smoke _ rings from _ the cor - ners of my mouth. _

Ducks and pigs and chick - ens call, _ an - i - mal car - pet wall to wall, _ A-
Hope the days that lie a - head _ bring us back to where they've led. _
Col - ored cot - tons hang in the air, charm - ing co - bras in the square, _

To Coda

1.
mer - i - can la - dies five foot tall in blue.
Lis - ten not to what's been said to
striped djel - le - bas we can wear at

2.

you.

Helplessly Hoping

Words and Music by Stephen Stills

Verse

2. Word - less - ly watch - ing, ___ he
3. Stand by the stair - way; ___ you'll

waits by the win - dow ___ and won - ders at the
see some - thing cer - tain ___ to tell you con - fu -

emp - ty place ___ in - side. ___
- sion has ___ its cost. ___

Heart - less - ly help - ing ___ him - self to her bad ___
Love is - n't ly - ing, ___ it's loose in a la -

___ dreams, he wor - ries: did he ___ hear a good - bye,
- dy who lin - gers, say - in' she is lost ___

Let chord ring.

21

Suite: Judy Blue Eyes

Words and Music by Stephen Stills

lis - ten to me, ba - by. _____ It's my heart _

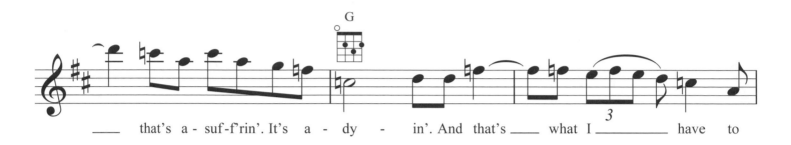

____ that's a - suf-f'rin'. It's a - dy - in'. And that's ____ what I _____ have to

lose. *(Instrumental)*

I've _____ got an an - swer. _____
Will _____ you come see _____ me

I'm _____ go - ing ___ to fly a - way. ____
Thurs - days _____ and Sat - ur - days? ____

What have I got to lose? _____
What have you got to lose? _____

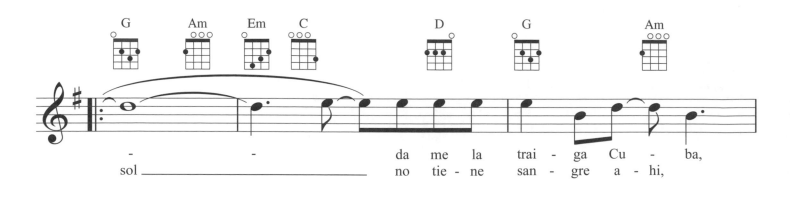

sol _____ no tie - ne san - gre a - hi,
- - da me la trai - ga Cu - ba,

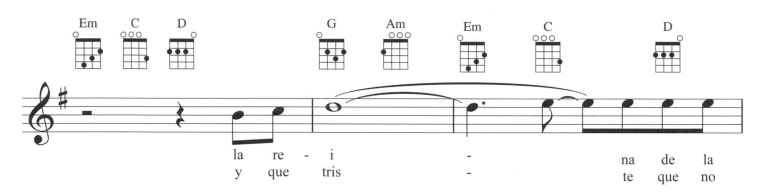

la re - i - na de la
y que tris - te que no

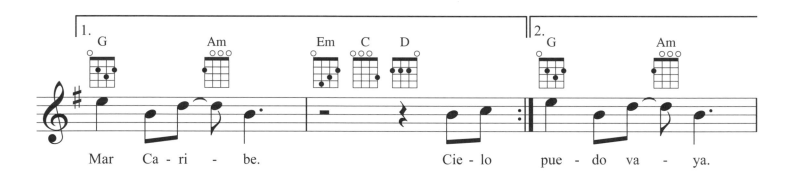

Mar Ca - ri - be.   Cie - lo pue - do va - ya.

Oh va! Oh va! Do do do do do, do   do   do do do do,

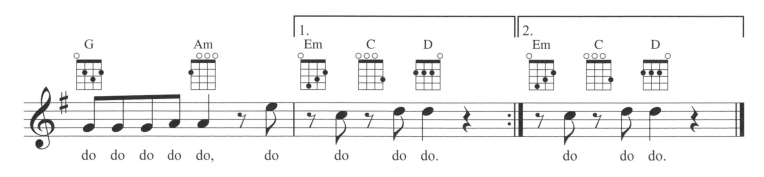

do do do do do, do   do   do do.   do   do do.

Our House

Words and Music by Graham Nash

used to be __ so hard. __ Now ev - 'ry - thing __ is eas - y 'cause of

(2nd time, rit.)

you   and   our...   La,   la,   la, la, la, la, la, __

__ la, la, la, la, __ la, la, la, la,   la,   la, la, la, la, __ la, la, __ la,

la, la, la, __ la, la, la, la, la.   la,   la, la, la, la, __ la, la, la.

Outro-Verse
Slower

I'll light the fi - re   while you place the flow - ers in the vase __

rit.

__ that you bought __   to - day. _____

31

Teach Your Children

Words and Music by Graham Nash

Teach .... your chil - dren well;
Teach .... your par - ents well;

their fa - ther's hell .... did slow - ly go ___
their chil - dren's hell .... will slow - ly go ___

___ by.
___ by.   And   feed

them on ___ your   dreams;   the one ___ they

pick's   the one ___ you'll   know ___   by. _____

___   Don't   you   ev - er   ask ___ them

why; if they told you, you __ would { die, cry, } so just

look at them __ and sigh _____

1.

and know they love _____ you.

2.

2. And love _____ you.

Let chord ring.

Additional Lyrics

2. And you of tender years
Can't know the fears that your elders grew by.
And so, please help them with your youth.
They seek the truth before they can die.

Southern Cross

Words and Music by Stephen Stills, Richard Curtis and Michael Curtis

Pre-Chorus

Think a - bout how man - y times

I have fall - en. Spir - its are

us - in' me, larg - er voic - es call - in'.

What heav - en brought you and me can - not be for - got -

- ten. I have been a -

Chorus

round _____ the world,

look - in' for that wom - an, girl who

knows __ love __ can en - dure, and you know it will. __

Interlude

3. When you see __
5. So we cheat -

Verse

__ the South - ern Cross for the first time,
- ed and we lied and we test - ed,

you un - der - stand __ now why you came __ this
and we nev - er failed __ to fail. It was the

way.
eas - i - est thing to do.

'Cause the truth you might __ be
You will ___ sur -

run - nin'   from   is   so   small,
vive   be - ing   best - ed.

but it's as
Some - bod - y

big   as   the   prom - ise,
fine   will   come a - long, make me for - get a - bout

the   prom - ise   of   a   com - in'
lov - in'

1.   N.C.   2.

day.
you

4. So _____ I'm

in   the   South - ern

Outro

Cross.

Wasted on the Way

Words and Music by Graham Nash

Wooden Ships

Words and Music by David Crosby, Stephen Stills and Paul Kantner

Say, can I have some of your pur-ple ber-ries? Yes, I've been eat-ing them ___ for six ___

___ or sev - en weeks now. Have-n't got sick once. Prob-'ly keep ___ us both ___

___ a - live. ___

Chorus

Wood-en ships on the wa - ter, ver-y ___ free ___ and eas-y.

Eas - y, you know the way ___ it's sup-posed to ___ be. ___

Sil - ver peo - ple on the shore-line, let us ___ be. ___ Talk-in' 'bout

very ___ free ___ and eas - y. ___

Chorus

Hor - ror grips us as ___ we ___ watch you ___ die. ___

All we can do is ech - o your ___ an - guished ___ cries, ___

stare as all hu - man feel - ings ___ die. ___ We are

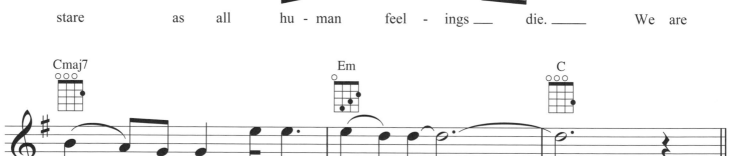

leav - ing; ___ you don't need ___ us. ___

Chorus

Go, take your sis - ter then by the ___ hand. ___

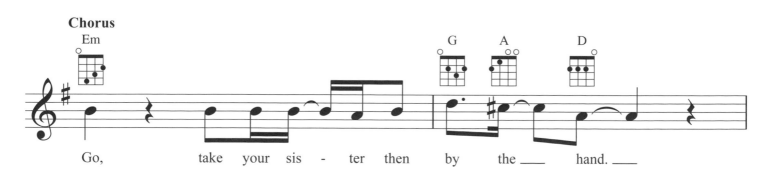

You Don't Have to Cry

Words and Music by Stephen Stills

First note

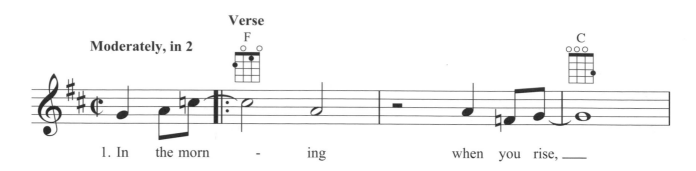

1. In the morn - ing when you rise, ___

do you think ___ of me, ___ and how ___ you left ___ me cry -

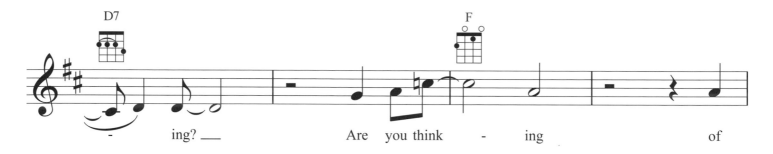

- ing? ___ Are you think - ing of

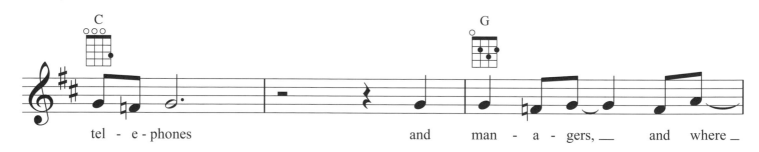

tel - e - phones and man - a - gers, ___ and where ___

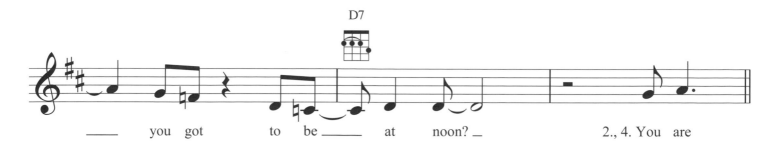

___ you got to be ___ at noon? ___ 2., 4. You are

Chorus

_____ have time _____ to cry, my ba - by. _____

You don't have _____ to cry. _____ I said cry, my ba -

- by, _____ you don't have _____ to cry. _____ I said

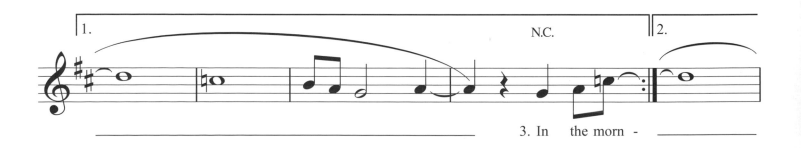

cry, my ba - by, _____ you don't have _____ to cry. _____

1.   N.C.   2.

3. In the morn - _____